LITTLE BENJAMIN AND THE FIRST CHRISTMAS

LUKE 2:1 – 18 FOR CHILDREN

Written by Betty Forell
Illustrated by Betty Wind

Benjamin watched the people coming into Bethlehem. What a lot of people there were! The king had ordered them to come to Bethlehem to be counted.

Some of them stayed in Benjamin's father's inn. Soon all the rooms were taken.

The inn was full of noise and excitement. "Here, boy, bring some hay for our donkeys!" they called out to Benjamin.

ARCH® Books

© 1964 CONCORDIA PUBLISHING HOUSE, ST. LOUIS, MISSOURI
CONCORDIA PUBLISHING HOUSE LTD., LONDON, E. C. 1
LIBRARY OF CONGRESS CATALOG CARD NO. 63-23146
MANUFACTURED IN THE UNITED STATES OF AMERICA
ALL RIGHTS RESERVED
ISBN 0-570-06005-2

Finally Father locked the gate. No more room. Not even a corner. The family was tired and hungry. Supper smelled good. Father led them in their evening prayers. He read from the great prophet Isaiah:

"The people who walked in darkness have seen a great light. . . . For to us a Child is born . . . the Prince of Peace."

Father told the children what the words meant. "God has promised to send us a very special Prince to rule over all people and save us from wars and bad kings. In His kingdom all people will live together in love and peace."

"When will this Prince come?" Benjamin sighed. "This is such an old promise from God. Will it ever come true? Will I ever get to see the wonderful Prince?"

Someone knocked on the door.

"No more room!" shouted Father.

Another knock. Father went to the door.
Outside stood a man and a woman.

"We are very tired," said the man. "We have walked a long way. Don't you have a little room for us?"

"No more room," said Father. Then Father had an idea. "I could let you sleep in the stable."

Benjamin went to show them the way.

Through the courtyard he guided them, past sleepy travelers, to the stable.

The animals in the stable looked up as they came in and watched Benjamin pile fresh hay in a corner for the man and woman to sleep on.

"What's your name?" the man asked him.

"Benjamin," he answered.

"My name is Joseph," said the man, "and this is Mary, my wife. It took us five days to get here from Nazareth on foot."

Soon the town quieted down. The weary visitors and the tired townspeople all slept.

Benjamin was dreaming of all the crowds he had
seen that day.

Suddenly, something awakened him. He ran to the window. A very bright star was rising in the sky. Everything was quiet except for the cry of a baby. But there was a light in the stable. Benjamin rubbed his eyes. Were there people going into the stable?

In a flash Benjamin slipped out of the room, out of the inn, out to the stable. There he saw an amazing sight.

On the hay which Benjamin himself
had put in the manger for the animals, lay a beautiful, newborn baby.
Mary and Joseph were watching
over the baby. And close by knelt a
group of shepherds.

"What are those shepherds doing here?" Benjamin asked himself. "And why are they kneeling?"

One of the shepherds beckoned to him. The shepherd was a rough-looking fel-low. Benjamin was just a bit afraid of him.

But the man said, "Come in and see! It's the Prince of Peace!" The man's voice was so full of wonder that Benjamin forgot his fear.

"A Prince?" Benjamin asked. "But He's just a baby and in a stable."

"As we were watching our sheep tonight," the shepherd said, "suddenly an angel came to us. We were terribly frightened. But then the angel said:

" 'Be not afraid . . . I bring you good news . . . for to you is born this day in the city of David a Savior, who is Christ the Lord. And this will be a sign for you: you will find a Babe . . . lying in a manger.'

"Then came many more angels, all singing praise to God.

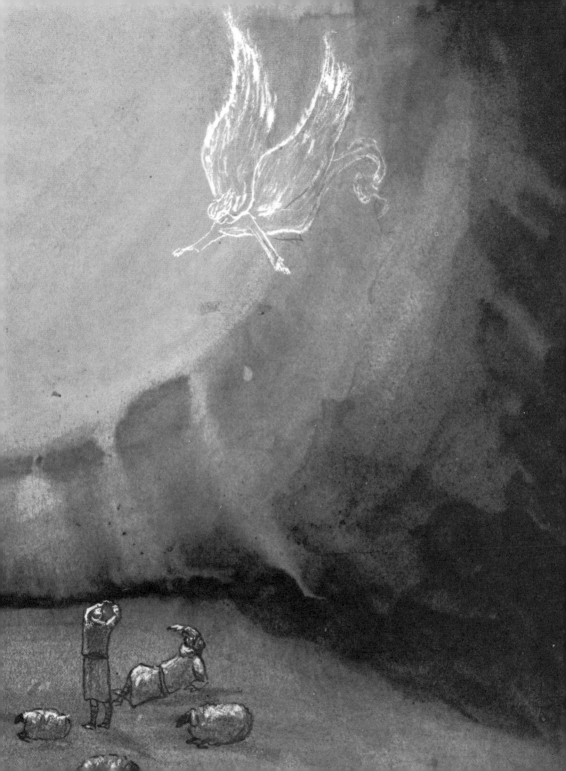

"As soon as they went away, we went and found this stable. Here is the Baby in a manger just as the angel said!"

So this Baby was the Savior, the Prince of Peace for whom Benjamin and his father and his grandfather and his great-grandfather had waited all these years. Benjamin stepped forward to see the little Christ Child better.

Then he knelt down. He thought of
what his father had read that evening:

"The people who walked in darkness
have seen a great light. . . . For to us a
Child is born . . . the Prince of Peace."

Dear Parents:

The story tries to tell about the coming of the Christ Child the way a small Jewish boy of Jesus' time would have seen it. It tries to show how very much and why he would have been waiting for it. It reminds us how he would have been surprised to see the great Prince Messiah, the Lord Christ, as a baby in the place where he put food each day for the domestic animals.

By and large the people of Jesus' day expected the Messiah, or the Lord Christ, to come with kingly power and glory. His coming as their humble brother went against all they had expected. God's ways are so different from ours.

One of the promises God made about the Messiah was that His would be a kingdom with true peace between men, nature, and God (Is. 9:6, 7; 11:1-10). There was no agreement among the Jewish people how this would come about. The New Testament sees the peace which God offers in Jesus Christ as the coming of the Messiah's kingdom of peace and the brotherly love in Christ's church as part of it. When Jesus returns in glory, all evil will be destroyed. Then the dream of Benjamin and of his father and grandfather will come true.

Can you help your child to see the true meaning of Christmas, with its wonder over the love of God which made the Lord Christ want to share the humblest and commonest way of life, the love which brings peace from God and makes peace among men possible? You may want to read to your child (or help him read it himself) the story of Jesus' birth in your Bible. (Luke 2:1-20)

The Editor